SPOTLIGHT ON ECOLOGY AND LIFE SCIENCE

THREATENED, ENDANGERED, AND EXTINCT SPECIES

WENDELL RHODES

PowerKiDS press™

NEW YORK

Published in 2017 by The Rosen Publishing Group, Inc.
29 East 21st Street, New York, NY 10010

Editor: Theresa Morlock
Book Design: Michael Flynn
Interior Layout: Mickey Harmon

Photo Credits: Cover (leaf texture) PremiumVector/Shutterstock.com; cover (image) Adam Jones/Getty Images; p. 5 (white rhino) JONATHAN PLEDGER/Shutterstock.com; p. 5 (Malayan tiger) lipik/Shutterstock.com; p. 5 (Siamese crocodile) PK.pawaris/Shutterstock.com; p. 7 (inset) JHU Sheridan Libraries/Gado/Contributor/Archive Photos/Getty Images; p. 7 (main) ittipon/Shutterstock.com; p. 8 https://meta.wikimedia.org/wiki/File:Bison_skull_pile.jpg; p. 9 robert cicchetti/Shutterstock.com; p. 11 (inset) Bob Rowan/Getty Images; p. 11 (main) Sacramento Bee/Contributor/Tribune News Service/Getty Images; p. 13 Mark Carwardine/Getty Images; p. 15 (main) GUDKOV ANDREY/Shutterstock.com; p. 16 LMspencer/Shutterstock.com; p. 17 PEDRO PARDO/Stringer/AFP/Getty Images; p. 19 Apic / Contributor/Getty Images; p. 20 pixelrain/Shutterstock.com; p. 21 RAUL ARBOLEDA/Stringer/AFP/Getty Images; p. 22 Stephen Simpson/ Getty Images.

Cataloging-in-Publication Data

Names: Rhodes, Wendell.
Title: Threatened, endangered, and extinct species / Wendell Rhodes.
Description: New York : PowerKids Press, 2017. | Series: Spotlight on ecology and life science | Includes index.
Identifiers: ISBN 9781499426007 (pbk.) | ISBN 9781499426038 (library bound) | ISBN 9781499426014 (6 pack)
Subjects: LCSH: Endangered species--Juvenile literature. | Extinct animals--Juvenile literature.
Classification: LCC QH75.R494 2017 | DDC 333.95'22--dc23

Manufactured in China

CPSIA Compliance Information: Batch #BW17PK For further information contact Rosen Publishing, New York, New York at 1-800-237-9932.

CONTENTS

ONE WORLD, MANY SPECIES

Humans are just one of the 8.7 million different **species** on Earth. Each species contributes to the world in its own way, and each member of an **ecosystem** provides **resources** for others. Without this range of species, all of Earth's ecosystems would suffer.

Nearly 24,000 species that we know of are endangered. This means that their populations are so low they're at risk of going extinct, or dying out completely. Around 26 percent of all mammals, 13 percent of birds, and 42 percent of amphibians are endangered. Nearly 12,000 species of plants, algae, and fungi are endangered.

The huge spike in the human population over the past few hundred years has resulted in plant and animal species going extinct faster than ever before. In this book we'll study how natural events and human activities have affected the animal species of our planet, and what can be done to protect them.

SIAMESE CROCODILE

MALAYAN TIGER

WHITE RHINO

In 1973, the Endangered Species Act was put into place to protect endangered species and their **habitats**.

CHAPTER TWO

NATURAL VS. UNNATURAL EXTINCTION

Once a species is extinct, it will never exist again. You probably know that dinosaurs once lived on Earth but are now extinct. The extinction of the dinosaurs may have been the result of natural climate changes. Many of the extinctions happening now are the result of human activities.

Habitat destruction is the leading cause of extinction. Natural habitats are destroyed when people use land to build homes, farms, and businesses. The more space humans take up, the less space there is for animals. Humans also create a lot of trash, which pollutes the **environment**. Pollution is also caused by the chemicals used in farming, mining, and **manufacturing**. People hunt and **exploit** certain animals for the **commodities** they provide. These activities are causing extinctions to happen much faster than they would naturally.

RACHEL CARSON

Biologist Rachel Carson spread awareness about the effects of pesticides, which are chemicals used on farms. Her book *Silent Spring* was published in 1962.

CHAPTER THREE

EXPLOITATION

Until laws were put into place to protect them, many species that are now endangered were once victims of exploitation. Exploiting an animal could mean mistreating it, harming it, or overhunting it.

During the 1800s, when many Americans began moving west, a great number of bison roamed the plains. Since bison need a lot of space to graze and roam, their habitats became very limited as people started to build railroads and homes. Some people hunted bison for the resources they could provide, such as hide, meat, and horns. Others hunted them for sport, killing many more than could be used. By the beginning of the 1900s, only about 300 bison were left in the wild. Bison are now protected from overhunting by the laws of the Endangered Species Act of 1973. They are considered a threatened species, but they're no longer endangered.

No other species population has dropped as quickly as the plains bison population did during the 1800s. The photograph on page 8 shows a pile of thousands of bison skulls in 1870.

CHAPTER FOUR

POACHING, PETS, AND PERSPECTIVE

Hunting wildlife illegally is known as poaching. People poach animals for commodities such as furs, horns, and ivory.

In some places, wild animals are captured and sold as exotic pets. Owners who don't know how to care for these animals may keep them in poor conditions. Although some exotic pets are legal to own, it might not be what's best for the animal.

An important issue in determining the future of endangered species is our perspective, or the way that we think about them. How do we decide the value of an animal's life? Is it only valuable if it provides commodities or services to people? Or is it valuable for its own sake? If we determine a creature's value based only on how we can use or sell it, we lose sight of its larger part in Earth's ecosystem.

WARNING

YOU ARE ENTERING A RARE OR
ENDANGERED SPECIES HABITAT.

WILLFUL DESTRUCTION OF A RARE OR
ENDANGERED SPECIES HABITAT IS A
VIOLATION OF FEDERAL LAW AND
MAY BE PUNISHABLE BY FINE OF UP TO
$10000 AND/OR IMPRISONMENT FOR
SIX MONTHS OR BOTH. (U.S.C. 1540).
STAY ON DESIGNATED ROADWAYS.

Wildlife sanctuaries are homes for animals that have lived in **captivity** in zoos or circuses or as exotic pets. Thika, Iringa, and Toka were three African elephants brought to Performing Animal Welfare Society's ARK 2000 Sanctuary.

CHAPTER FIVE

INTERDEPENDENCE

All living things are connected to each other through their ecosystem. Each member of the community relies on others to provide the resources it needs to survive. This is called interdependence. We can learn the consequences of extinction by thinking about the role of an endangered blue whale in its ecosystem.

Blue whales were once hunted almost to extinction because oil can be made from their blubber, or fat. Although it's now illegal to hunt blue whales, they're still threatened by pollution, shrinking habitats, and large ships, which can injure them.

Endangered blue whales eat tons of small creatures called krill each day. Without a predator to keep their population in check, krill could crowd out other species by using up too many resources. Whales also produce waste that provides **nutrients** to small animals lower in the food chain.

Blue whales are the largest animals in the world. One blue whale can weigh as much as 33 elephants.

CHAPTER SIX

CRITICALLY ENDANGERED SPECIES

Critically endangered species are those animals that face immediate risk of being wiped out. One example is the mountain gorilla. Gorillas are one of the human species' closest animal relatives. Other than chimpanzees and bonobos, gorillas share the most similarities with humans. Gorillas can laugh and make tools. They even look a lot like us.

Loss of habitat is the main cause of gorilla endangerment. Gorilla habitats are destroyed when people cut trees for wood, build mines to collect resources, or clear parts of the forest to build farms. This means that gorillas have fewer resources. They are also put at risk by human diseases, poaching, and the exotic pet trade. More than half of the mountain gorillas in the world now live in Virunga National Park in the Democratic Republic of the Congo, where agents are stationed to protect them.

For a long time gorillas were thought of as violent and brutal. In truth, gorillas are mostly peaceful.

CHAPTER SEVEN

LIVING IN CAPTIVITY

When a wild animal is kept in a zoo or aquarium, it's said to be living in captivity. Some endangered species are extinct in the wild and the only surviving members are in captivity.

If you've ever visited a zoo, you may have seen endangered animals there. Zoos were created as places for people to learn about animals from around the world. Scientists study the animals in zoos to learn about their behaviors. Some people feel that zoos are helpful to endangered animals because they protect living members and make sure new ones are born.

SAN DIEGO ZOO

This little cub was bred in captivity to help increase the population of the endangered jaguar species.

Captive breeding programs help endangered animals have babies in captivity. Sometimes animals born in captivity are later released in the wild. This is called reintroduction. Unfortunately, unless long-term habitat protection plans are put in place, species that are reintroduced may still die off quickly.

CHAPTER EIGHT

WHAT'S BEING DONE

The International Union for **Conservation** of Nature, more simply known as the IUCN, is a group of people from around the world who work together to protect the environment. The IUCN puts together a "Red List" of species that are at risk of endangerment or extinction.

Wildlife biologists and zoologists are scientists who research animal habitats, observe animal behaviors, and examine how humans affect animal species. The information collected by wildlife biologists and zoologists helps people know how to help species that are at risk of extinction. By understanding more about animals, their behaviors, and their needs, people can work more effectively to **restore** their habitats and populations. You can look up organizations like the World Wildlife Fund, National Wildlife Federation, and Defenders of Wildlife to find out more about endangered species and actions being taken to protect them.

Jane Goodall is a famous primatologist, which is a scientist who studies species of primates, or monkeys and apes. Goodall studies chimpanzees.

CHAPTER NINE

CONSERVATION AND PROTECTION

We think of animals as our workers, pets, predators, and prey. The first step in restoring endangered species is to respect animals as neighbors in our world community instead of seeing them as commodities.

An endangered red howler monkey is released into the wild in a protected forest area in Colombia.

To **ensure** the survival of endangered animal species, scientists are studying their behaviors, rebuilding and conserving their habitats, and helping put laws into place to prevent people from exploiting them. By defending habitats from pollution and land development we can make sure that the environment is healthy for future generations. An endangered species is considered restored when threats to its habitat and population have been reduced enough to allow it to survive in the wild.

National parks provide habitats for many endangered species whose homes have been destroyed by land development. Forest rangers, wildlife biologists, and environmental educators work every day to protect and promote wildlife and their habitats.

CHAPTER TEN

HOW YOU CAN HELP

There are many ways you can take part in the movement to protect endangered animals. Find out which plants are native to the area where you live and plant a few. Plants are a key part of the ecosystems that support all animals. You can protect animals from pollution by taking part in a community cleanup to pick up trash. If you'd like to support an organization that's working to protect endangered species, ask your parents if your family can make a donation.

Most importantly, learn more about endangered species and teach your friends what you know. Appreciating the world's amazing species and the important roles they play in the environment will inspire people to think more carefully about how their actions could affect these animals' survival.

GLOSSARY

captivity (kap-TIH-vuh-tee) For an animal, the state of living somewhere controlled by humans—such as in a zoo or an aquarium—instead of in the wild.

commodity (kuh-MAH-dih-tee) A raw material or product that can be bought and sold.

conservation (kahn-surh-VAY-shun) Efforts to care for the natural world.

ecosystem (EE-koh-sis-tuhm) A natural community of living and nonliving things.

ensure (en-SHUR) To make certain.

environment (ihn-VY-run-munt) The natural world around us.

exploit (eks-PLOYT) To treat something unfairly for one's own benefit.

habitat (HAA-buh-tat) The natural home for a plant, animal, or other living thing.

manufacturing (man-yoo-FAK-chur-ing) The process of making products on a large scale.

nutrient (NOO-tree-uhnt) Something taken in by a plant or animal that helps it grow and stay healthy.

resource (REE-sohrs) Something that can be used.

restore (ree-STOR) Returning something to its original state.

species (SPEE-sheez) A group of plants or animals that are all the same kind.

INDEX

PRIMARY SOURCE LIST

Page 7
Rachel Louise Carson, author of *Silent Spring*. Photograph. 1961. Now kept at the John Hopkins University Sheridan Libraries.

Page 8
A pile of American bison skulls waiting to be ground for fertilizer. Photograph. ca 1870. Now kept in the Burton Historical Collection, Detroit Public Library.

Page 19
Jane Goodall is shown at Gombe Stream National Park, Tanzania. Photograph. 1995.

WEBSITES

Due to the changing nature of Internet links, PowerKids Press has developed an online list of websites related to the subject of this book. This site is updated regularly. Please use this link to access the list: www.powerkidslinks.com/sels/threat